From an essay on clothing by Will McBride.

A Balinese father about to bury his child, from a Look essay on Southeast Asia by Paul Fusco.

the Photo Essay: Paul Fusco & Will McBride

text by Tom Moran
with the editors of Alskog, Inc.

An Alskog Book published with
Petersen Publishing Company,
Los Angeles, California

Prepared by Alskog, Inc.
Lawrence Schiller / Publisher
William Hopkins / Design Director
John Poppy / Executive Editor
Vincent Tajiri / Editorial Director
Julie Asher / Design Assistant
Arthur Gubernick / Production Consultant
Jim Cornfield / Technical Consultant

Petersen Publishing Company
R. E. Petersen / Chairman of the Board
F. R. Waingrow / President
Alan C. Hahn / Market Development Director

Photographic Publishing Group
Brent Salmon / Publisher
Paul Farber / Editor

Library of Congress Catalog Card Number: 74-80802
ISBN: 0-8227-0071-9
First Printing
Published simultaneously in Canada
Printed in the United States of America

Will McBride's opening photograph for an essay on new directions for human-kind.

From Fusco's Southeast Asia essay.

Introduction

An essay is one of the most personal and powerful forms of narration a photographer can use. Its series of images, telling a story along straightforward literary lines or resonating with each other to develop a theme in freer form, offers a visual adventure that is at once deep and broad.

People meet photographs every day as illustration, journalism, portraits, studies of the human figure in action, personal statements by well-known professionals. We see more photo essays in a day than we realize, in company slide presentations, TV commercials, and of course in magazines. The ordinary family photo album need not be what a famous essayist recently described to us as a "parking lot" of snapshots; instead, a summer vacation or a birthday party could be presented as a rich, rounded experience.

As the most contemporary of photographic forms, the essay is also the most controversial. What, exactly, *is* a photo essay? There was not much argument over definitions as the form matured during the 1930s and 1940s in the hands of pioneers such as Margaret Bourke-White, Leonard McCombe and W. Eugene Smith, who seems to have been the first to use the word "essay" to describe it. But now, in its second and third generations, there are probably as many definitions as there are photographers. Smith, author of not only the name but of the classic examples of one type of essay, leaves no doubt in this book about his own unyielding standard. There are those who will disagree with him. Amid the arguments, the photo essay is thriving in the hands of photographers such as Paul Fusco and Will McBride.

Fusco and McBride are poles apart as personalities and as story tellers, but both are photo essayists who repeatedly test new approaches and refine older ones. Fusco's concern for the real joys and problems of the people he photographs emerges through a working style that is basically exploration. He finds people he wants to photograph—farm workers, his children, Appalachian miners—and enters the flow of their lives, letting the truth, as he sees it, unfold before his camera.

McBride, on the other hand, works more like a film director. Often casting actors in his essays, he constructs a series of images worked out in advance. The essence of his work is fantasy; the intent is to persuade a viewer to try some course of action—to follow Hermann Hesse's Siddhartha or Europe's young vagabonds into a new way to live—and the main ingredient is a meticulous arrangement of beauty.

This book, itself an essay on essayists, owes much of its depth to the generous help of photographers including W. Eugene Smith and Bill Pierce; art directors including Allen Hurlburt and Will Hopkins; picture editors including John Durniak, Dick Pollard, and Charles Reynolds; and of course, Paul Fusco and Will McBride.

From a McBride essay on
love and war.

From one of Twen's many love stories by McBride.

people to give him reading lists and then plowed through every book they suggested. His work began to include visions of hope for a fuller future, a more joyful life. Fusco thinks of himself as a pessimist, ready to see the grimmer realities of the world, but this new view seemed worth a try. "I don't think we can hide the reality of life," he says, "but you do have to look for ways of presenting an alternative to what we have. It might be the wrong one, but you have to push here, take a look there. Maybe something will come of it."

The journalists **covering the emerging "human potential movement" began to see California as a laboratory of social and cultural change,** and Fusco's assignments began to take him frequently to the West Coast. He and his family would move from Manhattan to Mill Valley, near San Francisco, in 1970. A year before, they rented a summer house in the California beach town of Bolinas while Fusco worked on *Look*'s Seventies issue.

The intellectual part of the concept was clear enough: Humankind has a better chance than ever before to make a good life for itself, thanks to its ability to learn and to a technology that might be bent into helpful channels. But Fusco and the other members of the

team producing the issue spent hours searching for ways in which he could put a visual, emotional handle on the concept for 34 million readers wearied by the Vietnamese War, domestic assassinations and a sense of national uneasiness. Finally, they decided to start off by rekindling a sense of adventure. How to do that? What theme could possibly be universal enough to appeal to all segments of the mass audience?

Why not start at the most basic level, by rediscovering Earth itself? After all, the planet would still support its people generously if they just remembered to treat it with respect. But a collection of beautiful nature pictures would be a bore. The essay needed people. An approach emerged from all the talk: Fusco would construct a tale in which a pair of children find themselves set down on a planet that they see, for the first time, with clean eyes.

Now he could move. He wanted some control over his situations, but not so much that they would look stilted, so for models he turned to two children he could trust to gambol with no awe of the camera: his own.

The essay was well under way one evening when Fusco pushed his chair away from the family's dinner table. "Let's go up on the mountain," he said. "We'll see if there's any sun up there."

A blanket of chilling fog had hung over Bolinas all day, but he knew the peaks of the Coast Range often poked their heads above it. From checking the newspaper that morning, he also knew the sun was not due to set for

A Chance to Begin The Highest Human Adventure

BEYOND SURV

A future of inches, plodding step ahead of extinction, is no future. We cannot go that way signs instead, of the glory we almost in his grasp, look far beyond brute survival to the ingredients of hope we have gathered on the following 14 pages. a pla

TEXT BY JOHN POPPY   PHOTOGRAPHS BY PAUL FUSCO

A Planet washed by cool mysteries

Without the shield of its atmosphere and the healing wash of its seas, this would be a lifeless chunk of rock, swinging dumbly through lethal radiation in naked space like its sister planets, viciously dead cold. But Anthony and Maya, the mythic travelers, find a Pla

another hour. He and Marina, his nine-year-old daughter, drove up the road connecting their cottage with a flank of nearby Mount Tamalpais. As they broke into clear air, they both gasped.

The world seemed to be floating on a sea of creamy fog that was about to swallow the evening sun. Fusco had been to this spot many times and knew that some evening he would see such a thing, but he had never before seen it like this.

Incredible, he thought. Unbelievable. "How do you feel?" he asked Marina, watching as her young eyes took in a sight to which she could not respond with words.

"Do whatever you feel like," he told her. "Anything you want." Marina reacted by rolling in the high grass and then dashed off across the mountain's curved shoulder. As she played, he followed her with his Leica MP camera, shooting and waiting for the sun to drop lower in the west.

He would have only a few minutes at most to make the picture he wanted, and he might not see such a thing again before the deadline for the essay. An incident light meter gave him a quick reading of the sunshine falling where he stood. He had pulled from his bag a camera with a 21mm wide-angle lens to encompass the scene around Marina's running figure. With the camera's Leicavit rapid-wind attachment he could shoot almost as rapidly as if it had a motor.

Each time he made an exposure, he changed the aperture by half a stop to protect the picture, since he was not sure what lighting effect would most truly describe the emo-

tional content of the moment. No light meter, no matter how accurate, can interpret emotional impact. Under the strange backlighting atop the mountain, as he shot directly into a disappearing sun, he knew the meter could serve only as a basis for his own calculations. He bracketed by about three stops on each side of the meter reading, covering the full range of possibilities from dark silhouette to high-key overexposure.

Fusco did not know at the moment that he had just made the opening photograph of his essay, but he and the writer knew it a few weeks later when they saw the picture glowing up at them from his light table. They had already completed the second half of the essay, covering computers, nuclear reactors, rocket engines and other examples of technology (not shown here), so he continued his search with the children.

Marina and her brother Anthony, then 11, visited some of the most spectacular scenery in western America, from Pacific tide pools to Death Valley, the silvery ice caves of Mount Rainier and the Olympic rain forest. Fusco was bringing the children into contact with nature's brilliance, recording the meeting with his cameras.

At each stop, he trailed behind them and photographed their reactions. He never asked them for a specific pose or tried to coax them into an unnatural response. The reaction, the discovery, had to be their own. Yet Fusco was definitely the impetus for their being in such locales and his purpose was clear — to wait until the children's actions illustrated the pre-deter-

21

mined concept with which he was working.

Fusco's casual surface is deceptive, masking as it does the fierce attention to detail that makes him 10 times the technician anyone expects of a man with a tattered canvas bag containing several cameras so worn that the brass shines through the enamel on their bodies, a man who answers questions about technique with, "Oh, I don't think much about that kind of stuff after all this time." Pressed for details, he turns out to think quite a lot about it. When a situation is about to change and the light is difficult, technique can make the difference between communicating forcefully and missing the picture. "Getting command of the fundamentals of lighting, lenses, film and so on," Fusco says once he decides to talk about it, "frees you to concentrate on the content of a picture."

An example: The difference in light levels between inside and outside the Mount Rainier ice cave at the right was tremendous, but Fusco saved the picture he wanted by exposing for the sky outside, thus silhouetting the children — and covered himself by bracketing a little. A 21mm lens emphasized the eye-like opening of the cave, just as a 180mm

lens emphasized the bulk of the sand dune in its companion picture. "Things like inclines never look as big or steep as they really are unless you enhance the feeling with the lenses."

Fusco's equipment is very nearly an extension of his eye and hand. His basic arsenal consists of four 35mm cameras, each equipped with a lens of a different focal length: three Leicas for a 21mm, a 28mm and a 35mm, and a Nikon F for the 180mm lens. In his gadget bag he carries lenses for special situations, from a 15mm wide angle to a 400mm telephoto. On most jobs, however, he wants to record the action around him without interfering with it, so his four basic lenses stay on the same four camera bodies. Whether he is photographing his children at play on the planet, or a miner's plight in Kentucky (pages 40-47), this arrangement provides him with ready access to a camera and lens that will fit what he sees in front of him. Fusco finds the four lenses sufficient for most situations. Not only do they give him a number of ways to frame any subject, but carrying each one mounted on its own camera means he can make his choice fast; time spent removing and replacing lenses could mean missed pictures, and the commotion of all the changing around could distract a subject at close quarters.

To an essayist who might shoot hundreds of pictures for every one that finds its way into the final exhibit, 35mm cameras are indispensable. The Leica caused a revolution in photography when it was introduced to the public in 1925; its compactness, quick handling and 36-exposure film rolls

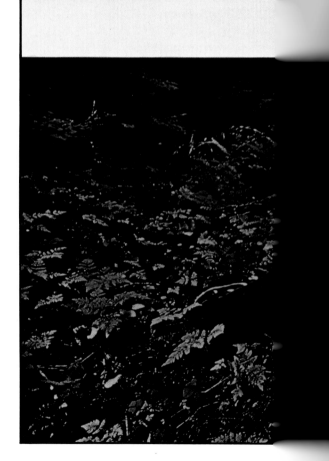

expanded the horizons of all photojournalists, whether they dealt with news pictures, portraits, sports, or essays. The quiet shutter helps Fusco avoid intruding on situations he wants to record. The rangefinder, allowing viewing and focusing through a clear window separate from the optical system of the lens, helps him work accurately in low-light situations that are sometimes difficult with through-the-lens systems.

On the other hand, the easiest way to see what you are going to get with a telephoto lens like Fusco's 180mm is to mount it on a single-lens reflex (SLR) camera like his Nikon, then frame and focus through the lens. The slightly louder noise an SLR mirror makes as it pivots out of the way for an exposure is no bother to a subject far away enough to call for a telephoto.

When he finished shooting the Seventies essay, Fusco stacked up boxes containing thousands of color transparencies and began sorting. Into the first discard pile went the missed moments and the culls from bracketing—bad exposures, an occasional shot in which the depth of field was not what he wanted. Although he shoots a lot, he concentrates on every frame, and there were surprisingly few mechanical rejects.

Next went the good exposures that, for one reason or another, did not fit the mood he wanted in the finished essay. Finally, narrowed down to a few hundred images, the take was ready to show to the writer and art director.

Fusco's tendency to "bracket, bracket the hell out of it" applies only to color essays, since his control over highlights, shadows and tones in a color picture is limited pretty much to the moment of exposure. If one portion of an otherwise good picture is underexposed, he cannot save it in a darkroom as he can a black-and-white print. That darkroom control made black and white the *vin ordinaire* of all early essays; Fusco and others still favor it for social documentation, where color would often be falsely gaudy, and for situations in which they must shoot when something happens, whether the light is good or not.

As he sorted, he did what he still does today, following the rigorous habits of his school days. He studied minute details in each picture as it went by.

His practice has not changed. Recently, Fusco sat hunched over the small light table in his converted garage. Unlike McBride and many other photographers who publish as widely as he does, Fusco has no studio, just a workroom. Photojournalists seldom maintain studios, since they spend the bulk of their time photographing the world outside, instead of a created environment inside. Behind him stood a row of file cabinets containing part of a life's work of slides and prints; the rest of his files are at Magnum, his agency, and the Library of Congress. He pressed his eye against the cup of a magnifying glass, peering at the details of each transparency in front of him. He pushed one away across the white surface, only to pull it back suddenly and search the image once more. This is a process of criticism, one whose reward might come the next time he picks up a camera.

Sharing human problems

Beyond the information they convey—does a coal miner's cabin have plumbing? What does the machine that took his job look like?—Fusco's best essays enfold a viewer in the emotional bond that develops between photographer and subject.

The jobs of families who had worked the coal veins of Appalachia for generations were being destroyed when Fusco arrived to report on the human costs of strip mining. Reproduced on these pages is a nine-page social document that journalism departments in a number of universities regard as a modern classic: an essay that presents the large theme of brutality in the name of profit, and flows from beginning to end as a story of one family's suffering.

Fusco made more than a thousand exposures. From them he selected

GEORGE'S BRANCH, KY.

Technical section

THE APPROACH

Every photo essay obviously begins with an idea. It can be generated by the photographer, a friend, a writer, an editor or an art director, but often it emerges from a pooling of several individual talents.

There are few ideas, if any, that cannot be represented visually, though some might take a great deal more planning and manipulation than others. In any case, the essayist aims to flesh out the idea by making a series of photographs that, when interwoven, will enlighten or move a viewer.

Whether a professional essayist is considered to be primarily a journalist or an illustrator, the germ of the idea can come from a news event (as in Paul Fusco's *La Causa*), a combination of social commentary and visionary themes (as in Will McBride's *The New Man* and Fusco's *George's Branch, Ky.*), or a single personality of great interest (McBride's *Adenauer* and Fusco's *Diana Ross*). An amateur can look to family, vacations, friends, neighborhood, and other subjects of special importance, and then arrange pictures in an album in exactly the same way a professional might arrange them in a magazine.

From the beginning of his career at *Look* magazine, Fusco would spend his early morning hours

reading the New York *Times* from cover to cover. One of the things he was looking for was news items that could become picture essays. In 1968 he read an article on a Kentucky coal-mining company that was automating and cutting down its payroll. The plight of the unemployed coal miner was a subject about which Fusco felt deeply. He based his presentation of the idea to his editors not only on his personal interest but also on the relevance of the theme to the current American situation. Two days later, a writer was assigned to accompany Fusco on the project that produced the essay on George's Branch (pages 40-47).

Will McBride and Willy Fleckhaus, *Twen* magazine's art director, spent many hours discussing the ways in which they saw society changing and their ideas about contemporary attitudes and mores. In the course of one of these conversations, Fleckhaus gave McBride a copy of a novel that was enjoying tremendous popularity among young readers, Hermann Hesse's *Siddhartha,* and before the photographer finished reading it he had begun sketching picture possibilities in the margins. McBride was convinced that he had to illustrate the book's message photographically. Fleckhaus agreed, with a canny eye on his magazine's youthful audience, and McBride was soon on his way to India to work on a complex essay that bears his strong personal stamp (pages 60-62).

Once a suitable subject has been selected, the photographer must decide on an approach that will most strikingly illustrate his discoveries and his feelings about them. There is no standard personal or technical approach, no pattern that will always work. Each situation generates an approach that suits what the photographer wants to say.

The able photographer must see what is unique about his subject, analyze the circumstances and the action taking place before the camera, and decide on a way to transmit them to a viewer. Of the many ways to look at a complex experience, the seasoned professional usually finds one that sums up the truth of the situation as he or she sees it.

Fusco prefers an open approach, working from a base consciously devoid of preconception, gaining his understanding by observing subjects as he photographs them. He develops a thematic structure and does much of his research while he works with his cameras.

McBride is most comfortable studying the theme he will work on before he actually begins photographing it, sketching out picture possibilities, designing a shooting script, detailing needed props, actors and makeup before he picks up camera or light meter.

Yet a measure of the success of both these photographers is their versatility, their ability to adapt an approach to the subject at hand, to concentrate on organizing an essay that illuminates the subject instead of obscuring it, and to speak with distinct visual impact.

In order to translate these concepts into photographs, the first and most important consideration for both Fusco and McBride is an understanding of the tools and techniques at their command.

THE IMPORTANT OPENING PICTURE

The most important photograph in any essay is the one designated as the "opener" or "lead" picture. A photographer engaged in a photo essay or picture story searches constantly for the one image that will:

• Intrigue the viewer, attracting intellectual and emotional interest to the story, and

• Introduce the viewer immediately and succinctly to the theme and major elements of the story.

Many of McBride's essays deal with abstract ideas, subjects that do not lend themselves to a linear progression of narrative pictures. He therefore finds it especially important to make an initial photograph that is graphically strong and dramatic enough not just to capture the viewer's attention, but also to prepare for subsequent exposition and sub-themes.

McBride's opening photograph for the essay called *Der Neue Mensch* is an excellent example of a powerful opener. The theme of the essay centers around the new perceptions, attitudes and life-styles of young people. They live in a world that many perceive as more complicated than it was in the past, and McBride wished to show how they might come into harmony with it through simplicity and independent values. As he sees it, the most staggering of the many aspects of modern life is its reliance on technology. People who begin to feel overcome by mechanization and supercomputers begin to fear they are losing control over their lives. McBride sought to allay those fears with an image suggesting that technology, being a product of human intellect and creativity, can harmonize with humankind itself.

McBride used a television set to symbolize the products of modern technology, and decided to cradle the small-screen receiver in the arm of a man whose physical strength would seem to overwhelm any threat the TV might offer. On the screen, an eye serves as a reminder of the humanity behind technology. McBride used a portable Sony TV camera to transmit the image of the eye to the screen, focusing the closed-circuit camera's zoom lens on a female model on whom he had trained a floodlight from the side. The transmission was live, simultaneous with the taking of the still picture.

McBride placed the male model holding the TV set in front of a spun-glass screen that he uses frequently to form a luminous, diffused background in the studio. A single electronic flash, behind and very close to the translucent spun glass, provided a soft light that was strong around the head and upper torso and then fell off rapidly into darkness. A second strobe, aimed into a reflector umbrella, was placed directly behind the still camera and aimed downward from a height of about seven feet to provide frontal illumination.

In retrospect, McBride feels the lighting on the eye could have been simpler, with the floodlight at the front, instead of the side, to tone down the abruptness of the shadows.

To synchronize the exposure with the rate at which a TV electron gun constructs an image as it scans lines on a screen, McBride used a shutter speed of 1/30 second — "or maybe even 1/15 second in this case" — stopping the lens aperture down to f/8. The camera for this picture was a Pentax Spotmatic equipped with a Zeiss Jena Flektagon 20mm wide-angle lens that served to emphasize the breadth of the male model's shoulders and the bulk of his arms, subduing the power of the technological symbol.

As we will see later, McBride admired the opti-

74

cal qualities of the Flekta-gon — an East German lens —but no longer uses it because it was so fragile that it kept breaking. He used the single-lens reflex Pentax to take advantage of its through-the-lens viewing and focusing, because the composition of his close-up pictures is often so precise that he cannot afford even the slight parallax of a rangefinder camera. The difference between the view of an object as seen through the picture-taking lens and the view as seen through the separate range-finder could throw off his framing by crucial inches.

Fusco operates differently, of course, when reporting on lives that he intends to show as they were before he arrived. Still, the importance of the essay's opening photograph can bring him out of hiding, no matter how much he wants to avoid interfering with his subjects.

Fusco tried to be as unobtrusive as he possibly could while doing his essay on George's Branch, yet in his quest for an opening picture he had to ask Mary and Rado Combs to pose for him. Looking for "a Grant Wood squareness and symmetry," he asked them to stand by a window in their house for a portrait

(page 40, inset). Here he used his 180mm lens on a Nikon F, from a distance of about 30 feet. The ground dropped off below the window, so he had to back up to a rise in order to stand nearly level with the subjects; a shorter, wider-angle lens would have included too much surrounding detail and destroyed the simplicity he wanted to use in setting the emotional tone for the remainder of the essay. Fusco used the Plus-X film that he always uses for outdoor black-and-white work, over-exposing by half a stop to make sure he got good shadow detail in the faces and bodies behind the glass, where he expected the light to fall off. His exposure was 1/125 second at f/5.6.

THE TELEPHOTO AS A TOOL

Individual photographs in an essay must complement each other, each adding to the narrative and emotional impact of the

others. Yet each can stand as a dramatic picture, an individual statement, in itself. Paul Fusco's photograph of a young miner waiting for his wife (pages 40-41) is an excellent example.

When he saw the young coal miner waiting on the road below the house of his father-in-law, Fusco wanted the picture but did not want to destroy the emotional atmosphere by charging out the back door, circling the house and running up to his quarry. Instead, he slipped out the doorway onto a front porch and began taking photographs with a tool made for just such situations, a 180mm lens. The miner, again some 30 feet away, paid scant attention to the photographer and Fusco was able to capture the anxiety and fatigue emanating from the man. He used a shutter speed of 1/250 second, fast enough to avoid softening the critical sharpness of the image with camera movement— one of the great hazards of telephoto lenses.

Long focal-length lenses contribute to the essayist's versatility. If Mahomet—or Fusco or McBride—cannot go to the mountain, the telephoto can bring the mountain to him.

Fusco used the telephoto again in the tableau combining a trio of United Farm Worker pickets with a mobile shrine in the greyness of an early morning fog (pages 32-33). The purpose here was manifold. By putting distance between himself and his subject matter, he shot through more layers of fog than if he had stood close, and therefore emphasized the lonely, quiet mood he felt in the moment. Also, the long lens "flattened" the planes of the picture by compressing front-to-back perspective, adding to the symbolic, almost icon-like quality of the composition.

The advantages of the telephoto lens do not come without the need for care.

Generally speaking, the longer the focal length, the longer and heavier will be the lens itself, and the greater the necessity for discipline in camera technique. Camera steadiness becomes imperative. Since the 180mm, f/2.8 Elmarit that Fusco uses has an angle of view of only 14 degrees as compared to the 46 degrees of a 50mm lens, a slight movement of his camera could be translated into the equivalent of several feet of movement by the subject—and as much as one-eighth of an inch on the film plane. It goes without saying that the result would be a blurred image.

Because of this, some professionals use tripods or special shoulder-chest braces to insure themselves against camera movement when using extreme telephotos. Up to 180mm or slightly longer, however, Fusco usually hand-holds.

Since longer lenses have less depth of field than short ones, they can be used to isolate a prime subject from its surroundings. By focusing sharply on the subject and working with as wide an aperture as possible, a photographer can throw foreground and background out of focus, thus subjugating distracting or meaningless elements into inoffensive blotches and blurs.

Another ideal use of lenses longer than the "normal" is portraiture. Will McBride used a 90mm telephoto for his tightly cropped candid portrait of Konrad Adenauer on pages 84-85, and for his posed portrait of a young Indian woman in profile (bottom left, page 61) for his Siddhartha essay.

The latter photograph, made in an improvised studio in Benares, India, was lighted almost identically to the photograph of the male model holding a TV set that led off Der Neue Mensch, except that the backdrop was an orange sari draped from a horizontal bamboo rod several feet away from a white wall. McBride put one Braun Hobby Strobe behind the cloth; another bounced light onto the front of her profile from a white umbrella behind and slightly above the camera.

McBride, of course, uses long lenses much less frequently than Fusco. His true dedication is to the wide-angle lens, as you can see by studying his Siddhartha essay.

THE WIDE-ANGLE AS INTERPRETER

Will McBride's visual interpretation of Hermann Hesse's Siddhartha was an undertaking almost as massive as a motion picture production. In pursuit of the photographs he had visualized for the story, McBride shot thousands. With very few exceptions, all of them were made with wide-angle lenses varying only four millimeters in focal length: the 20mm and 24mm Jena-made Zeiss Flektagons, lenses that are no longer obtainable.

McBride learned to swear by, and to swear at, the Flektagons. He loved the fact that he could move in as close as 10 inches to his subject when focusing and that, for wide-angle lenses, the Flektagons' linear distortion was minimal. Nevertheless, he found them to be extremely delicate; their moving parts broke easily, so he had to buy three lenses at once to be sure he had one that was working whenever the others fell apart.

After Siddhartha he gave up on the fragile Flektagons and has switched over completely to the products of Ernst Leitz; his lenses are Summicrons, Super Angulons and Elmarits, fitted to Leica and Leicaflex bodies. McBride recognizes that lower-priced equipment would last the lifetime of most amateurs, but knows that professional use and abuse makes top-grade equipment not a luxury but a necessity for him.

Whether the optics come from East German Jena glass, from the "rare earth" of Japan, or from Wetzlar in West Germany, all photojournalists and photo essayists rely heavily on wide-angle lenses. They often need an angle of view that can be as wide as 94 degrees for a 20mm lens or 81 degrees for a 25mm, compared to the 46 degrees of the standard 50mm. Coupled with such peripheral vision is the wide-angle's great depth of field—which, among other advantages, relieves the

Will McBride's Leicaflex with all the standard lenses
The Leicaflex SL and six of its family of R lenses. From left to right: 35mm f/2.8 Elmarit-R; 21mm f/4 Super Angulon-R; 50mm f/2 Summicron-R (on camera); 90mm f/2.8 Elmarit-R; 180mm f/2.8 Elmarit-R; and the 135mm f/2.8 Elmarit-R.

General Uses of Telephoto							
Type of Photography	**Telephoto Lens**						
	85	105	135	180/200	300	400	600
Portraiture	▓	▓	▓				
Sports/Action		▓	▓	▓	▓		
News Coverage			▓	▓			
Theatre		▓		▓	▓		
Landscapes		▓		▓			
Wildlife				▓	▓	▓	▓

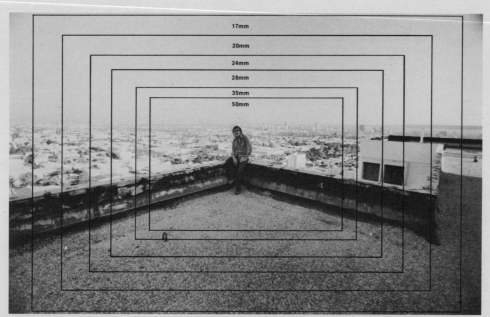

17mm
20mm
24mm
28mm
35mm
50mm

The fields of view that lenses of differing focal lengths cover at a distance of 25 feet from the subject.

photographer of some focusing problems. Once a wide-angle is focused on a subject 10 feet away, for example, with the aperture set at mid-range, re-focusing is almost unnecessary unless the subject moves many yards.

"The simpler the technique I use," McBride says in this connection, "the nearer I am able to stay to the things going on and the more I can concentrate on the revealing of truth and the relating of experiences." As he has said in talking about the shooting of *Siddhartha,* the use of wide-angles draws him into the picture in a way that involves a great deal of forward movement of his body; not only is he moving in toward the subject, but he is also adding or subtracting elements with these slight changes of position.

While telephoto lenses tend to compress space, almost eliminating the illusion of dimension in a photograph, wide-angles work the other way around—they magnify apparent depth. Objects in the foreground seem to project themselves toward the camera, while

76

those farther away shrink away. The resulting visual effect can help a photographer create dramatic sculptural compositions.

An excellent example of the unique characteristics of the wide-angle is the photograph on pages 56-57 of the young Siddhartha meditating. McBride spent several days studying the many temples of the holy city of Benares until he found one that would be ideal for the picture he had in mind. After receiving permission to photograph inside the temple, he and his crew began to set up for shooting in the early predawn hours; a previous check of the location had shown him exactly how the rays of the rising sun would come through the windows behind his model, and exactly what pattern the light would make. He then used the extreme curvature of a 20mm Flektagon to emphasize the center foreground of the picture, both by making portions of the model's body seem to project forward and by making objects near the edges of the frame seem to lean away. The eye follows all these lines to the boy's center—which, for a Buddhist, is where it should go.

The kind of light a photographer likes to work with often influences his style

and the look of his pictures. Most photographers try to avoid the harshness of mid-day sunshine; beyond that, McBride shows a preference for soft daylight and seldom makes pictures in direct sun if he can avoid it.

When he could not shoot in early morning or late afternoon, he used other devices in *Siddhartha* to rid himself of raw sunlight that was not softened by clouds or haze. He shot in shaded areas, or at right angles to the light, or straight into it, using subjects' bodies to mask the sun itself from the lens.

The *Siddhartha* series shows some of the hazards that wide-angles bring to such shooting, as well as McBride's way of using them to his advantage instead of fighting them. In the photograph of the two boys in the water at the bottom left of page 60, the sun —outside the frame at the top—reflects on the water to cause a "flare-out" that destroys the silhouette of the boy at the left. At the top left of page 61, in a picture for which McBride used a 20mm lens to photograph two boys with three tiny men framed between the legs of one of them, the flare-out occurs over the right angle made by the knee even though the sun was out of the frame.

In both photographs, McBride used the flare to convey a feeling of heat and intense sunlight. A photograph on page 60 of Siddhartha holding religious scrolls shows another use for the flares that a wide-angle's curved glass tends to pick up. Here, the sun-spots grow progressively larger as they extend upward from the scroll, ending in a large spot of light in the middle of the model's head—a simple, direct way for McBride to suggest the progression of wisdom from one repository to another.

But flares are not always welcome. To avoid their ever-present danger when working outdoors with wide-angle lenses, both McBride and Fusco carry lens shades as important accessories. Each type of wide-angle requires its own specific shade; a shade made for a lens longer than the one to which it is attached will cut into the field of view, eliminating part of the photograph. Unless such "vignetting" is done deliberately, it has about the same appeal as a thumb over the lens.

DEPTH OF FIELD

One technique that both Fusco and McBride use to emphasize the things they find important in a picture is careful manipulation of the sharpness of objects at different distances from the lens.

A single-lens reflex camera allows a photographer to check this depth of field directly by pushing a "preview" button that stops the lens down to a preselected aperture setting and shows the area of sharpness in the pentaprism viewfinder.

The clear window of a rangefinder camera, however, does not offer such information; everything appears in sharp focus. While depth-of-field numbers are etched next to the focusing ring on all lenses, the numbers make sense only if a photographer un-

HOW LENS OPENINGS AFFECT DEPTH OF FIELD

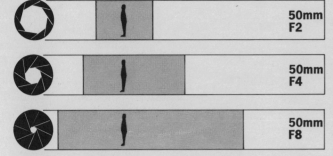

50mm F2

50mm F4

50mm F8

HOW SUBJECT DISTANCE AFFECTS DEPTH OF FIELD

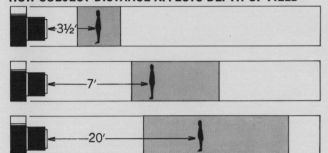

3½'

7'

20'

HOW FOCAL LENGTH AFFECTS DEPTH OF FIELD

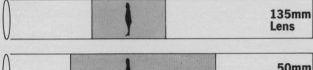

135mm Lens

50mm Lens

24mm Lens

derstands how depth of field can be affected by three factors: lens aperture, focal length of the lens, and distance at which the lens is focused.

This chart gives an idea of how depth of field changes with each.

BRACKETING

If Paul Fusco had to condense his advice on photographing in color to one word, it would be "Bracket!"

He shoots color at the exposure his meter tells him to, then at shutter speeds and f/ stops above and below it—not because he is unsure of what he is doing but because such bracketing is one of the few ways he can control the emotional information in a color picture. Given a black-and-white negative, he can work for hours in a dark-room to make precisely the

print he wants; he cannot do that with a color transparency. Once he presses the shutter release with color film in the camera, the only thing left to do is to drop it off at a lab for developing.

Bracketing does, of course, provide some insurance against varying light conditions, inconsistencies in meter readings, or variations in color-film emulsions. Beyond that, however, both Fusco and McBride know that the mood of a color picture can change drastically with very slight variations in hue and intensity. For Fusco, who shoots most often in situations where he does not control the light—only what he does with it—bracketing provides a chance to catch, perhaps on one frame of an entire roll, precisely the atmosphere he felt as the ex-

perience unfolded.

He bracketed every one of the exposures that went into his Seventies essay on the re-discovery of our natural environment (pages 18-25). He would take a meter reading and begin shooting at the indicated exposure. After clicking off several shots, he would move up or down a half-stop or a stop and continue until, in exceptional situations, the original exposure had been bracketed by as much as two full stops each way. He tends to bracket toward shorter exposures and smaller openings, since he leans toward underexposure and its increased color saturation on the transparency.

Bracketing can be done by changing the lens aperture, the shutter speed or both. Which to change? That depends on the sub-

ject matter and the aspect of the photograph that the photographer most wants to control.

Fusco's poetic seascape on pages 24-25 is an example of bracketing by changing shutter speeds. He did it that way not only to obtain different intensities of light as the sun set over the Pacific Ocean, but also to get different qualities of blur in the water flowing over the rocks. Wanting to convey his impression of the twisting, flowing channels of foam, he found himself working in one of those many instances in which an exposure meter could never tell him what to do.

On the other hand, he did his bracketing with the aperture setting for the photograph of the Mount Rainier ice cave on pages 22-23. The difference in meter readings from the

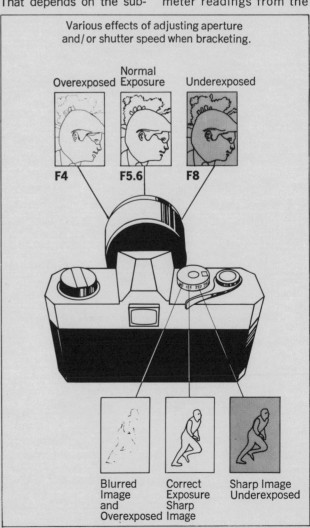

Various effects of adjusting aperture and/or shutter speed when bracketing.

Overexposed — F4

Normal Exposure — F5.6

Underexposed — F8

Blurred Image and Overexposed

Correct Exposure Sharp Image

Sharp Image Underexposed

dark interior of the cave to the sunlit clouds at its entrance was huge, so Fusco started from his highest meter reading, exposing for the bright background, and worked his way down the scale to a probable overexposure. He varied apertures to give himself a choice of color intensities and shadow details, keeping the silhouetted figures sharply outlined by adjusting his focus as the changes in aperture changed the depth of field. As a result, different frames showed different degrees of sharpness in the foreground; the transparency Fusco selected for publication retained sharpness from front to back, indicating that it must have been one of his smaller aperture settings.

PRINTING

When Fusco works in black and white, on the other hand, he knows that the process of creating a photograph might just be *starting* as he trips the shutter release.

And creating it can be, almost as much as in the making of a painting. Black-and-white film gives any photographer a latitude in exposure and a flexibility in the darkroom that color positive transparencies cannot match. Some of today's best photographers owe their understanding of the possibilities in their pictures—of the dimensions, the depth, the expressive potentialities of a photograph—to their background in black-and-white darkroom work.

Why? Simply because a black-and-white negative in a darkroom finally escapes the machinery where it has been imprisoned behind glass, metal, springs and knobs. An amazing number of photographers who have not spent an apprenticeship in a darkroom see picture-taking in terms of cameras, lenses, the hardware that transmits an image to the eye—an image that they often perceive only dimly as a meter read-

ing and a shape or two.

While the film is in the camera, a photographer can manipulate light only in a crude way, by letting more of it or less of it through the lens. He cannot reach in and hold his finger in front of a portion of the frame to subtract light from a too-bright face, say, nor can he expose just one dim corner longer than the rest of the frame. When the negative enters the darkroom, however, all those limitations fall away. The photographer can interfere with the light shining through his negative in the most minute, intricate, subtle ways, one square millimeter at a time if he wants.

When Fusco took the picture of Rado Combs' daughter and her miner husband walking up the curving road (pages 46-47), he knew he would not be finished with it until long after the shutter clicked. From the moment he aimed his camera at the couple, he knew the picture would require a great deal of darkroom

work to make it say to a *Look* reader what the scene said to him, but he could not sacrifice the shot. The road, the curve in its path, the bend in the miner's backbone, the set of his wife's shoulders, all indicated to Fusco an endless path, a journey with no rainbows in sight.

The hues of the dirt road and the vegetation surrounding it could have stood out from each other on color film, but Fusco's eye—trained in years of converting color mentally to the grey tonal scale of black-and-white film—told him that the color-blindness of the Plus-X film in his camera could make no distinction between these hues. They would register as very similar intensities of grey. At the moment, there was little he could do about that. He decided to

---

Notes for making a print on multi-contrast enlarging paper, using different filters to bring out contrast.

expose for the darkest areas, to hold detail in the shadows. If he had exposed for highlights (the road, in this case), the shadow areas would have gone almost black, blocking out detail. His exposure gave him something on the negative to work with. If detail exists, you can labor over a print to preserve it; if it doesn't, there is nothing you can do to put it in.

Fusco, like any other photographer working seriously in black and white, has learned to evaluate pictures in shades of grey before opening the shutter. With foreknowledge of what the final print will look like, he can make compensations on the all-important negative from which the print must be made. As he aims the camera, he has two alternatives: to vary exposures, or to use filters to lighten or darken specific areas. Judgments made at this point can save hours of darkroom time.

Even with advance knowledge of the problems of merging greys, a photographer frequently has no chance to select the proper filter and attach it over his lens; the instant available to him has to be devoted to exposure calculation, focusing and framing. As a photojournalist, Fusco seldom has time for filters, and he did not on this afternoon in Kentucky. To bring out the precise separation in tonal values he wanted in the figures on the road, he later spent hours in the darkroom, working on the print.

Before he started, Fusco had added yet another decision to his long list of choices: the type of photographic paper on which he planned to make the enlargement. He had basically two types from which to choose: *graded* paper and *multi-contrast* paper. Each type gives the photographer a different kind of control over the contrast—the range of tones from bright whites to deep blacks—in a picture.

Graded papers, usually numbered from No. 1 to No. 6, have emulsions that produce predictably different amounts of contrast in prints, depending on the grade used. The higher the number, the higher the contrast across the entire print made on a sheet of that paper. Had Fusco tried to print his low-contrast negative on a sheet of No. 1 paper, the result would have been a blob of almost uniform grey, with no highlights and no shadows. A "normal" print comes from balancing high and low contrast, so he might have tried printing on No. 4, 5, or even No. 6, all considered high-contrast papers; but as he worked his way up the scale, he would have produced increasingly harsh effects that did not fairly represent the melancholy light of the moment he had recorded. Besides, he saw several different contrast ranges within the single negative. No single grade of paper could handle them all.

The *multi-contrast* paper to which Fusco turned has not one emulsion on each sheet but two—a high-contrast one and a low-contrast one. Each responds to a different color of light coming from the enlarger. A set of special filters allows the photographer to produce different blends of the two colors, thus producing several different grades of print contrast on a single sheet of paper. Working on duPont Varigam, one of a number of brands of multi-contrast paper on the market, Fusco used different filters for different sections of the print, exposing small areas at a time on the enlarging easel. He "dodged" areas that were too dark, one section at a time, and "burned in" lighter areas such as the road to keep good detail.

Burning and dodging require only the simplest tools. For burning, Fusco usually cuts a hole in a piece of cardboard, then holds it under the enlarger so that extra light strikes the paper through the hole just where he wants the image to be darker. For dodging, he withholds light from part of the image with a solid piece of cardboard, or with his hand. In either case, he keeps the burner or the dodger moving so that its silhouette does not show up in the final print.

"The reason for spending all that time printing," he points out, "is not so that somebody will say, 'Wow, what a nice print!' Most of the people who look at the picture don't know a thing about printing and couldn't care less, and that's fine. But they see *something*, and they get a certain emotional punch from it, depending on how well you have made the print transmit the information you want it to. You have to control the print the same way a painter controls a painting, control the total sur-face." Using another analogy, he adds, "Taking a good picture and then not bothering to make a good print gets in the way of what you're trying to tell people; it's like saying, 'Well, I could have a great poem here but I don't feel like rewriting it.'"

THE ART DIRECTOR

But how do all those individual pictures find their way onto a printed page where they can interrelate with each other and tell their story?

Fusco's experience as a staff photographer at *Look* was quite different from McBride's at *Twen*. The two organizations had different personalities: *Look* was an informal, highly collaborative system in which photographers, writers, and art directors worked together to contribute to a statement

Will McBride's final layout for his children's sex book.

they all had a hand in, whereas *Twen* was more an autocracy run by the art director alone. While Willy Fleckhaus' power at *Twen* was unusual—he could arrange to have editors fired —the feeling among photographers today, since the folding of big staff-oriented picture magazines such as *Life* and *Look,* is that it is getting more and more difficult to retain control of essay layouts; perhaps the major area in which a photographer still enjoys the give-and-take that Fusco knew at *Look* is in book publishing.

When Fusco finished an assignment for *Look,* he would return to the magazine's offices and await the processing of the film. When the contact sheets (for black and white) or transparencies (for color) were ready, he would begin scanning images, doing his preliminary edit of a "take" that might amount to a hundred or more pictures for every one that would even-

tually be printed.

Then, if he was working with a writer who cared enough about the pictures to want a say in how they would be used, the two would join forces for further editing. The writer might bring his or her own needs to the process, judging the story-telling content of the pictures with an eye to the way they would work with the text being drafted; perhaps Fusco and the writer would disagree on the esthetic or narrative quality of one picture or another. Eventually, they would compromise, narrowing their "selects" down to 50-150 images. If they were in black and white, Fusco would then order 5x7 working prints, enlargements on which no remedial printing work would be done. If the selects were in color, he would load them into a Kodak Carousel tray, ready for projection.

At this point, the art director—Allen Hurlburt in Fusco's early days at *Look,* Will Hopkins later—would enter the scene. The three partners in the essay would go over the selected images, with Fusco and the writer

explaining them to the art director as they went along. Again, the selection of images to run in the magazine was a matter of debate; each of the three expressed viewpoints based on personal reactions to each picture and personal judgments of which combinations of pictures would serve the essay best. The final culling of the take might leave 10 to 20 photographs. It then became the art director's job, with Fusco and the writer looking over his shoulder at every step, to lay out the photographs in a way that would draw a reader into the experience of the essay.

When Will McBride finished an assignment for *Twen,* on the other hand, he would return the exposed film to art director Willy Fleckhaus with little or no pre-editing. One of his major grievances against periodicals is that so often—at *Twen, Quick,* and others—the record of his experiences became subject at a crucial point to the decisions of another person. The jeopardy here, he feels, is the possibility of misinterpretations and mis-

applications, no matter how deeply he respects the talents of a friend like Fleckhaus.

One layout that does please McBride, of course, is the one he did himself for the *Zoom* magazine version of *Siddhartha* (pages 60-62).

The role of the art director at a magazine depends greatly on the structure of the organization and the personality and strengths of the people in the editorial hierarchy. At a publication run by a strong, picture-knowledgeable editor, the art director might be little more than a competent designer who works with photographs selected for him. In other publications, the system might be more democratic, with assignments and final selections being made—as at *Look*—after those involved had voiced their opinions.

Regardless of power, the final responsibility for the appearance of a book or magazine, and the design of each page within it, belongs to the art director. That responsibility cannot help affecting the layout of an individual essay by any photographer who wants to be published—either by causing conflict, if the photographer's ideas clash violently with the art director's, or by bringing on a collaboration that might or might not improve the essay.

An amateur photographer who wants to assemble pictures into essays, in an album or a scrapbook, can pick up a number of useful ideas by studying layouts in the major magazines of today and yesterday.

McBride and assistants review first layouts of a newspaper he intends to publish.

In Aguascalientes, Fusco photographed the aftermath of a bullfight for an essay on Mexico. For the photograph on pages 82-83, he panned a 180mm lens with the victim of the fight as mules dragged it away.

auer's features, showing a man both rugged and vulnerable as he met with reporters for a farewell party (pages 86-87), walked through his garden south of Bonn (pages 88-89), and sat alone at last.

In 1965, two years before Adenauer's death, McBride's book-length portrait was published. The flow of its black-and-white images revealed not only a photojournalist's skill, but also a young man's admiration for the power of age. McBride puts it simply: "Almost every picture I take is of a person I like, a person I can identify with."

Just as McBride can abandon manipulation to make an essay of candid photographs, Paul Fusco can turn from his own working habits to direct a series of illustrations for a show-business personality story.

His challenge in photographing singer Diana Ross was a familiar one. Well-known performers are already shaped in the public mind as ready-made images; their

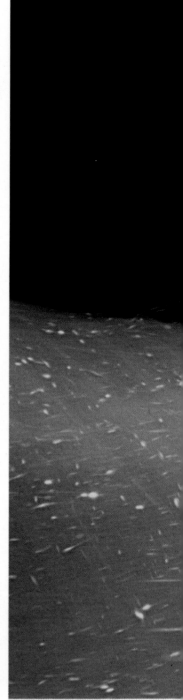